SADDLEBACK
EDUCATIONAL PUBLISHING

Descriptive ✓
Expository ✓
Narrative ✓
Persuasive ✓

DESCRIPTIVE
Writing

by EMILY HUTCHINSON

—— Writing 4 TITLES ——

Descriptive Writing
Expository Writing
Narrative Writing
Persuasive Writing

Development and Production: Laurel Associates, Inc.
Cover Design: Image Quest, Inc.

 SADDLEBACK
EDUCATIONAL PUBLISHING

Three Watson
Irvine, CA 92618-2767
Website: www.sdlback.com

Copyright © 2005 by Saddleback Educational Publishing. All rights reserved. No part of this book may be reproduced in any form or by any means, electronic or mechanical, including photocopying, recording, or by any information storage and retrieval system, without the written permission of the publisher.

ISBN-10: 1-56254-754-2
ISBN-13: 978-1-56254-754-7
eBook: 978-1-60291-544-2

Printed in the United States of America
11 10 09 08 07   9 8 7 6 5 4 3 2

Contents

To the Student

How about it? Can you count on your writing skills to make your meaning clear?

Check yourself out by answering the following questions!

▶ Can you give other people easy-to-follow directions and explanations?

    EXAMPLES: **how to tape a TV show**
                      how a bill becomes law

▶ Can you describe something clearly enough to create a vivid image in the minds of your audience?

    EXAMPLES: **a dramatic thunderstorm**
                      a movie star's mansion

▶ Can you tell a story so well that your audience is fascinated from beginning to end?

    EXAMPLES: **the history of baseball**
                      the world's worst date

▶ Can you usually persuade others to accept your opinion or take some kind of action?

    EXAMPLES: **see a certain movie**
                      register to vote

Saddleback's WRITING 4 series will improve your written work—
no matter what your purpose is for writing. If you make your best
effort, the result will surprise you. You'll discover that putting words
on paper isn't that much different from saying words out loud. The
thought processes and grammatical structures are the same. Writing
is just another form of expression; skill develops with practice!

Competent writers do better at school and at work. Keep that in mind
as you work your way through these books. If you learn to write well,
you're more likely to succeed in whatever you want to do!

*Are you ready to go for it?
Follow me—I'm off and running!*

Using Vivid Nouns

Nouns are words that name persons, places, things, or events. Good writers choose nouns that are specific rather than general. The word *dog*, for example, does not give the reader an exact mental picture. A specific noun such as *whippet, greyhound, dalmatian,* or *cocker spaniel* would create a much more precise image.

A. Rewrite each sentence, replacing the underlined word with a more specific noun that creates a clearer picture.

1. Please pass the <u>vegetables</u>.

   _____

2. We went to a <u>restaurant</u> for dinner on Saturday.

   _____

3. After dinner, we split a <u>dessert</u>.

   _____

4. Patrick bought a new <u>car</u>.

   _____

5. Jean lives in a <u>place</u> with an ocean view.

   _____

6. The <u>game</u> started at 3 o'clock.

   _____

7. We saw an interesting <u>animal</u> at the zoo.

   _____

8. Tom and Bob fished from a <u>boat</u>.

   _____

9. Gloria's <u>pet</u> is cute and friendly.

   _____

10. The <u>machine</u> made a lot of noise.

   _____

B. This picture shows a typical day in a park. Suppose you want to describe this scene to someone else. Where would you start? You might begin with vivid nouns. Make a list of nouns that could be used in a description of this picture.

_____   _____   _____

_____   _____   _____

_____   _____   _____

C. Now use some or all of the nouns you listed to write a description of the picture. Make sure your nouns are specific enough to help your reader visualize the scene.

Using Vivid Verbs

Good writers use strong, specific verbs to express action. Why? Precise verbs make it easier for the reader to imagine the action. Sometimes, strong verbs can give clues about a character's motivations or feelings. To see how a vivid verb can clarify meaning and bring a picture into focus, compare these two sentences:

> *The football team came onto the field for their final game.*
> *The football team bolted onto the field for their final game.*

Notice that the verb *bolted* gives the reader a sense of the players' determination. It also helps you imagine how emotionally charged up the team was.

A. Rewrite each of the following sentences, replacing the underlined word with a more vivid verb.

1. The couple <u>moved</u> on the dance floor.

   _____

2. Allan <u>went</u> out the front door.

   _____

3. Barbara <u>got</u> out of bed at 6 o'clock in the morning.

   _____

4. The child <u>walked</u> through the rain puddles.

   _____

5. The lioness <u>looked</u> for a meal for her family.

   _____

6. Chris <u>drank</u> a glass of ice water.

   _____

7. The fat cat <u>slept</u> by the fire.

   _____

8. All of a sudden, the police <u>came</u> in the door.

   _____

9. The out-of-control car <u>went</u> into the concrete wall.

   _____

10. The hungry man <u>ate</u> a sandwich.

    _____

B. This picture shows a typical scene at a circus. Suppose you want to describe the picture to someone else. Where would you start? You might begin with vivid verbs. Make a list of verbs that could be used in a description of this picture.

_____ _____ _____

_____ _____ _____

_____ _____ _____

_____ _____ _____

C. Now use some or all of the verbs you listed in a written description of the picture. Make sure your verbs are specific enough to help your reader visualize the scene.

Lesson 3 — Using Vivid Adjectives

Adjectives are words that give more information about nouns or pronouns. Writers use adjectives to describe colors, shapes, and sizes as well as tastes, sounds, smells, and feelings. Read the two example sentences. Notice how adjectives help the reader visualize what is being described:

> *Isabel purchased a thick green blanket.*
>
> *Myron served a hearty vegetable stew.*

A. Read each sentence. First, circle all adjectives that describe colors, shapes, or sizes. Then rewrite each sentence, changing the adjectives to create a very different visual picture. The first one has been done for you.

1. Daria wore a (shimmery) (pastel) shawl.

   Daria wore a tattered brown shawl.

2. Dennis painted a large red flower on the round canvas.

   _____

3. The bright blue butterfly hovered over the delicate white orchids.

   _____

4. Rocko is a tiny white puppy.

   _____

B. Read each sentence. First, circle all adjectives that describe sounds, tastes, smells, or feelings. Then rewrite each sentence, changing the adjectives to create a very different visual picture.

1. The noisy children played in the fragrant garden.

   _____

2. The hungry man wolfed down the spicy enchiladas.

   _____

3. Maria was too tired to enjoy the festive celebration.

   _____

4. A quiet hush fell over the mournful crowd.

   _____

C. This picture shows a typical scene at a campsite. Suppose you want to describe the picture to someone else. Where would you start? You might begin with vivid adjectives. Make a list of adjectives that could be used in a description of this picture.

_____ _____ _____

_____ _____ _____

_____ _____ _____

_____ _____ _____

D. Now use some or all of the adjectives you listed in a written description of the picture. Make sure your adjectives are specific enough to help your reader visualize the scene.

_____

_____

_____

_____

_____

_____

_____

_____

_____

_____

_____

_____

Developing an Outline

An *outline* is the framework for a planned composition. A writer creates an outline to plan and organize the major and minor points to be covered in the completed composition.

A. To show what you know about writing an outline, use words from the box to complete the sentences. Hint: You will *not* use all the words.

sketchy	detailed	write	rearrange	brief	type
review	structured	minor	separate	order	draft
details	sequence	plan	thoughts	topics	original

An outline is simply a _____. It helps you organize your _____ in the most effective _____. The better your outline, the easier it will be to write your first _____.

Outlines vary with the _____ of writing you are doing. An appropriate outline for a research project would be quite _____ and _____. For a one-page business letter, a fairly _____ and _____ outline will usually be adequate. But whether your outline is long or short, it will always set out the major _____ and the supporting _____ for each topic.

_____ your outline after you complete it. Be flexible. You may want to _____ the major sections or add something you didn't think of the first time around. Once you're satisfied that the major and _____ points are covered, you are ready to _____.

B. Write **T** or **F** to show whether each statement is *true* or *false*.

1. _____ Details in an outline might sometimes be called *subtopics*.

2. _____ The length of an outline should be tailored to the task at hand.

3. _____ An outline topic may be a phrase rather than a complete sentence.

4. _____ Each supporting detail must be a separate paragraph in your composition.

C. Suppose you've been assigned to write a three-paragraph composition. Use the items in the list to organize a topic outline. First, find the title and write it on the line. Next, pick out the three main topics. Then, fill in two subtopics for each main topic.

Arriving on time	**Applying for the job**	**The interview**
Over the telephone	**Creating the proper image**	**Part-time jobs**
Hearing about jobs	**Newspaper classified ads**	**Finding a Job**
from friends	**Letter of application**	

                                                _____

    I. _____

        A. _____

        B. _____

   II. _____

        A. _____

        B. _____

  III. _____

        A. _____

        B. _____

D. Now write an outline for a three-paragraph paper on one of the following subjects:

Common Courtesy	**Popular Music**	**Buying a Dog**

                                                _____

    I. _____

        A. _____

        B. _____

   II. _____

        A. _____

        B. _____

  III. _____

        A. _____

        B. _____

Using Vivid Adverbs

Adverbs are words that describe verbs, adjectives, and other adverbs. Writers use adverbs to describe actions and to tell *how, when,* or *why* something happened. Adverbs are also used to tell *how often* or *how much.* Read the three example sentences. Notice how adverbs help the reader visualize what is being described.

> *The waves crashed loudly on the shore.*
>
> *Dina walks on the beach late in the afternoon.*
>
> *The canary sang sweetly.*

A. Read each sentence. First, circle the adverbs that tell how, when, or why. Then rewrite each sentence, changing the adverbs to create a very different visual picture or meaning.

1. Jean gracefully skated across the ice.

   _____

2. Afterwards, we all enjoyed a cup of cocoa.

   _____

3. Breathlessly, Mona arrived at the station five minutes late.

   _____

4. Jeff was broke; consequently, he could not join the club.

   _____

B. Read each sentence. First, circle the adverbs that describe sounds, tastes, smells, and feelings. Then rewrite each sentence, changing the adverbs to create a very different visual picture.

1. Patrick writes checks biweekly to pay his bills.

   _____

2. Amber is extremely patient with her little sister.

   _____

3. Dennis hardly recognized his old friend.

   _____

4. Roxy performed her dance routine skillfully.

   _____

C. This picture shows a scene from the Old West. Suppose you want to describe this picture to someone else. Where would you start? You might begin with vivid adverbs. Make a list of adverbs that could be used in a description of this picture.

_____   _____   _____

_____   _____   _____

_____   _____   _____

_____   _____   _____

D. Now use some or all of the adverbs you listed in a written description of the picture. Make sure your adverbs are specific enough to help your reader visualize the scene.

_____

_____

_____

_____

_____

_____

_____

_____

_____

_____

_____

An *eyewitness report* often includes descriptive details that paint a clear picture of the experience. Someone who was *not* present at the scene couldn't provide as many accurate details. That's why reporters like to interview eyewitnesses. No other source can be so reliable.

A. Suppose you were present when a firefighter performed a heroic rescue. What might you have seen, heard, and smelled that day? Now put yourself in the place of the following characters. Write two sentences that each one might have said about the rescue.

1. a child rescued after being trapped in a smoke-filled room

_____

_____

_____

_____

2. the firefighter who dashed into a burning building and made the rescue

_____

_____

_____

_____

3. a neighbor who called the fire department

_____

_____

_____

_____

4. the parent of a rescued child

_____

_____

_____

_____

5. a passerby who stopped to watch the rescue effort

_____

_____

_____

_____

6. a firefighter who helped in the rescue

_____

_____

_____

_____

B. Now, choose one of the characters involved in the rescue. Write an eyewitness account from that person's point of view. Tell the story from beginning to end, being sure to include sensory details. Consider questions such as these:

- How did the smoke look and smell?

- What kinds of expressions did you see on people's faces?

- What sounds were made by the fire, the fire truck, the firefighters, the other witnesses, and the victims?

Eyewitness: Fashion Show

Have you ever been to a fashion show? Perhaps it was a fundraiser for a local charity or a show put on by a department store to promote a certain line of clothing. The rich and famous preview elegant new styles at *haute couture* shows in Europe and New York. Certain elements are present in all shows. There are always models wearing various styles of clothing, an announcer describing the clothing, and, usually, an opportunity to buy the clothing.

A. Read the following descriptions of fashion shows. Then write two sentences that you might include in an eyewitness report about it.

1. a fashion show put on by students in a sewing class

   _____

   _____

   _____

   _____

2. a show whose purpose is to sell prom wear

   _____

   _____

   _____

   _____

3. a bridal fashion show

   _____

   _____

   _____

   _____

4. a famous designer's high-style show in New York City or Milan, Italy

   _____

   _____

   _____

   _____

5. a show put on by a church guild to raise money for the day-care center

_____

_____

_____

_____

6. a fashion show highlighting sportswear of various kinds

_____

_____

_____

_____

B. Now, choose one of the fashion shows described in Part A, or make up one of your own. Write an eyewitness account of the show. Describe the event from beginning to end. Answer questions like these:

- What kind of clothing styles did you see?

- What unusual fabrics or colors were used?

- How would you describe the models' looks and attitudes?

- What outfit did you like best? Explain what you liked about it.

- Who was in the audience? Did they seem to appreciate the clothes?

- What kind of music accompanied the show?

_____

_____

_____

_____

_____

_____

_____

_____

_____

_____

_____

_____

Sentence Structure

Sentences that are varied in length, structure, and word order add interest and emphasis to writing. Study these examples of different sentence structures.

A **simple sentence** consists of one independent clause and no additional clauses.	⟷	*We went out for pizza.*
A **compound sentence** consists of two or more independent, or main, clauses.	⟷	*We went out for pizza and they watched a movie.*
A **complex sentence** consists of one independent clause and one or more dependent, or subordinate, clauses.	⟷	*Before we went out for pizza, we finished our homework.*
A **compound-complex** sentence consists of at least two independent clauses and one or more dependent clauses.	⟷	*We went out for pizza and they watched a movie as heavy rain pelted the city streets.*

A. Write **T** or **F** to show whether each statement is *true* or *false.*

1. _____ All clauses contain both a subject and a verb.

2. _____ A main clause is also called a subordinate clause.

3. _____ A main clause can stand alone as a sentence.

4. _____ *While the sun was shining* is an independent clause.

5. _____ A clause may also be called a phrase.

6. _____ *Scissors cut paper* is an independent clause.

7. _____ *Ray swam laps and Greg did stretching exercises while the coach was on the telephone* is a compound-complex sentence.

8. _____ *Weightlifting builds strength, but aerobic exercise results in more complete conditioning* is a complex sentence.

9. _____ *Fifty young soldiers, sailors, and marines marched in the big parade* is a compound-complex sentence.

10. _____ *The title of my favorite movie* is a dependent clause because it lacks a subject.

B. Use any of the four sentence structures to combine each group of sentences into one. Then name the sentence structure you used.

1. *The cat was chasing the mouse. The mouse ran into a hole in the wall. The cat was frustrated.*

_____

_____

_____ STRUCTURE: _____

2. *The telephone rang. Bill answered it. The caller was his girlfriend.*

_____

_____

_____ STRUCTURE: _____

3. *Nicole and Brad plan their vacation. They decide to visit Japan. They will go in April.*

_____

_____

_____ STRUCTURE: _____

4. *The store was very crowded. One customer was irate. She'd been waiting in line for 20 minutes.*

_____

_____

_____ STRUCTURE: _____

C. Now write an example sentence of your own to illustrate each structure.

1. **SIMPLE SENTENCE:** _____

2. **COMPOUND SENTENCE:** _____

_____

3. **COMPLEX SENTENCE:** _____

_____

4. **COMPOUND-COMPLEX SENTENCE:** _____

_____

Lesson 7 — Eyewitness: Moon Landing

What would it be like to visit the moon? Eyewitnesses to moon landings have described their experience. But you can use your imagination to envision it for yourself. Pictures sent back from the moon can help you fill in details. Recordings of astronauts' voices from outer space can help spark your imagination as well.

As you imagine a moon landing, you might wish to add an element of science fiction: What if some creatures were living on the moon? How would they view the astronauts who had landed on the surface of their world?

What unusual sights would you see on the moon? What would your hopes and fears be?

A. Think about those questions as you describe a moon landing from each of the following points of view.

1. the astronaut who steps out of the landing module

_____

_____

_____

2. the astronaut who places a flag on the moon's surface

_____

_____

_____

3. a creature who lives on the moon

_____

_____

_____

4. a scientist back on Earth who worked on the project

_____

_____

_____

5. an astronaut's spouse, watching the moon landing on a TV monitor

_____

_____

_____

6. a tourist who was brought along for the historic ride

_____

_____

_____

B. Now, choose one of the characters described in Part A, or make up a different character. Write an eyewitness account of the moon landing from that character's point of view. Describe the event from beginning to end. Answer questions like these:

- What is your mood as you observe the event? Are you frightened, excited, proud?
- What sounds can you hear?

- What does the moon look like from the surface?
- What does the Earth look like from the moon?

- What does it feel like to be nearly weightless?
- Were any unexpected difficulties encountered during the trip?

_____

_____

_____

_____

_____

_____

_____

_____

_____

_____

_____

_____

_____

Lesson 8 — Clothing of the Future

One thing you can say about clothing fashion is this: It changes! Take a look at fashions from other centuries, even other decades, and you'll see quite a difference. The clothing your grandparents wore when they were young was not a bit like what you're wearing now. And you can be sure that your own grandchildren's fashions will be different, too!

Designers aren't responsible for all changes in clothing styles. Cultural attitudes and available materials also have an influence. For example, winter clothing is much more lightweight now than it was in the past. Why? New and improved fabrics have been developed that keep us warm with less bulk.

A. With a little imagination, you can visualize fashions of the future. Compare them to past and present fashion by completing this chart. Consider style, fabric, and function. As an example, the first one has been *started* for you.

	PAST	PRESENT	FUTURE
SCHOOL CLOTHES	knee-length skirts in hard-to-clean fabrics	above-the-knee skirts in washable fabrics	skirts of any length in wear-once-and-throw-away fabrics
SHOES			
RUNNING GEAR			
SWIM WEAR			
EVENING WEAR			

B. Write a description of a future wardrobe. Include information about when and where the clothing would be used and why it is appropriate for that use.

For example, would an outfit be worn indoors or outdoors? Is it casual wear or formal wear? What is unusual about the design, color, or fabric?

On a separate piece of paper, make an illustration of the clothing you describe.

AVAILABLE NOW! LATEST FASHIONS FROM EARTH

Lesson 9 Story Settings

A story's *setting* is its time and place. Setting is a very important story element, for the plot and characters are often driven by it. Setting influences the cultural values of the characters as well as how those characters might behave within their culture. It can also determine what trials the characters might have to overcome.

For example, compare a character in medieval England with a character in modern America. Who would be more adversely affected by an infected tooth, a cold winter, or a meager harvest? Obviously, such trials would be harder in medieval times. When you write a story, you must keep the setting in mind. Characters and plot events must synchronize with the setting.

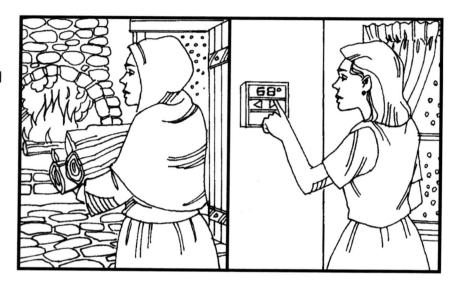

A. Consider each setting. Then write a few sentences describing what action each of the following characters might take next.

1. Caleb, who lives in New York in 2005, wants to meet his friend Sally for lunch. How will he explain to her where to meet, what transportation to take, and what they will eat?

_____

_____

_____

_____

_____

2. It's 1860. Abby is a slave who lives on a plantation in the state of Georgia. Along with a small group of other slaves, she wants to escape. How will group members discuss where to meet, how they will travel, and what they will eat?

_____

_____

_____

_____

_____

B. Read the lists of possible characters, settings, and plot events in the chart. Then mix and match to come up with a scenario of your own. For example, you might choose a father of six who lives in 1865 in South America and wants to build a new house. Next, write a paragraph describing an event in the life of your character. Be sure that the plot is consistent with the setting!

CHARACTER	SETTING: TIME	SETTING: PLACE
16-year-old girl	prehistoric era	Europe
24-year-old man	200 B.C.	North America
4-year-old boy	50 A.D.	South America
32-year-old woman	200 A.D.	Africa
young mother	1200	Australia
father of six	1500	Middle East
retired athlete	1602	India
tribal hunter	1776	Arctic region
research scientist	1812	desert
astronaut	1969	mountains
business owner	1998	tropical island
dancer	2010	big city
factory worker	2500	rural area

Usage: Formal and Informal English

Just as your choice of clothing varies depending on the situation, so can your speech and writing. Depending on your audience and purpose, you decide whether to use informal English or formal English. What is the difference? The everyday language you use when speaking is informal English. In informal writing, you can use contractions and slang, although you must still follow the standard rules of grammar, spelling, and punctuation. Informal English is appropriate for writing dialogue, stories, personal essays, poems, letters to friends, and journal entries. Here is an example of informal English:

> *I've never seen fans so crazy about their team. They couldn't sit still! It was fun to see them all psyched up about every play.*

Formal English is best used for serious purposes. These include essays, newspaper articles, formal reports, letters of application, speeches, and most school assignments. Here is an example of formal English:

> *The first time a hot-air balloon took to the air with passengers was in 1783. The Montgolfier brothers, its inventors, sent a sheep, a rooster, and a duck into the sky over Versailles for eight minutes.*

A. Read each of these passages. Write *formal English* or *informal English* to identify its style.

1. _____ Two dishes the Japanese prepare using raw fish are sushi and sashimi.

2. _____ Todd gets grossed out at the idea of eating raw fish.

3. _____ To make sushi, small pieces of raw fish are wrapped up with rice in dried seaweed.

4. _____ Sashimi is made from thin slivers of raw fish. I'd rather eat sashimi than sushi any day.

5. _____ Soy sauce and wasabi, a type of Japanese horseradish, are the usual accompaniments to sushi and sashimi.

6. _____ I tried wasabi once and, boy, was I sorry!

7. _____ Wasabi is a *very* hot condiment.

8. _____ The hostess led the young couple to their seats at the sushi bar.

B. This picture shows a typical scene in a gym. The scene can be described in formal or informal English. Write three sentences in informal English to describe what is happening. Then, write three sentences in formal English to describe the same thing.

INFORMAL ENGLISH:

1. _____

2. _____

3. _____

FORMAL ENGLISH:

1. _____

2. _____

3. _____

C. Now, describe what you like to do for exercise. Imagine two different audiences: a friend and a doctor. Use appropriate language for each situation.

TO A FRIEND:

_____

_____

_____

TO A DOCTOR:

_____

_____

_____

Lesson 10 · Describing a Mood

We express our moods—feelings—in many ways, including body language, facial expressions, and sounds. When describing someone's mood, a good writer describes the way that person looks or acts. In other words, a good writer *shows* the reader how the person feels rather than simply *telling* how the person feels. Notice the difference:

Telling about a mood: Julie was delighted.

Showing a mood: A smile slowly formed on Julie's face as she opened the brightly wrapped package and saw a new party dress. When she tried it on, her eyes sparkled with delight.

A. Improve on each of these descriptions by *showing* how the person looked or behaved. Write two sentences for each item.

1. Dave was frightened.

_____

_____

2. Carla was nervous.

_____

_____

3. Caleb felt ill.

_____

_____

4. Jerome was joyful.

_____

_____

5. Diane felt embarrassed.

_____

_____

6. Phyllis was enthusiastic.

_____

_____

B. Choose three of the moods listed in the box. Write a paragraph for each one, describing how someone expressed that mood.

proud	unhappy	playful	excited	hungry	stingy
lonely	neglected	suspicious	curious	unsure	playful
bored	flirtatious	apprehensive	generous	gloomy	fearful

MOOD: _____

DESCRIPTION: _____

_____

_____

_____

_____

_____

MOOD: _____

DESCRIPTION: _____

_____

_____

_____

_____

_____

MOOD: _____

DESCRIPTION: _____

_____

_____

_____

_____

_____

Lesson 11 — Thoughts of a Pet

Pets depend on their owners for all the necessities of life—food, shelter, health care, hygiene, and companionship. Imagine getting into the mind of a pet to find out its thoughts. It would be interesting to know what a pet thinks of its owner.

Do dogs really worship and adore the humans who take care of them?

Are cats really as aloof as they seem?

What probably goes through the minds of our other pets, such as reptiles, birds, and fish?

A. To loosen up your imagination, envision yourself in each animal's place. What would you be thinking? Write your thoughts on the lines.

1. A dog notices that his food bowl is still empty when it's an hour past his usual feeding time.

   _____

   _____

2. A cat is having her coat brushed by her owner.

   _____

   _____

3. A new bird has just been added to a large cage crowded with other birds.

   _____

   _____

4. A turtle is picked up and carried away by the toddler in the house.

   _____

   _____

5. A rabbit is munching on a carrot provided by his owner.

   _____

   _____

6. A goldfish senses that the filter in the aquarium isn't working properly.

   _____

   _____

7. A dog takes his leash to its owner, hoping to be taken out for a walk.

   _____

   _____

8. As if watching his private TV set, a cat stares at the caged birds.

   _____

   _____

B. Now, choose one of the pets described in Part A, and write a story that continues the description. What happened next, and then after that? What did the pet think as each event happened? How did the owner behave?

_____

_____

_____

_____

_____

_____

_____

_____

_____

_____

_____

_____

_____

_____

Lesson 12 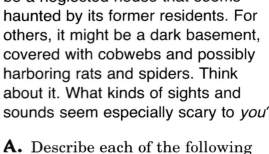 A Scary Place

What is the scariest place you can imagine? For some people, it might be a neglected house that seems haunted by its former residents. For others, it might be a dark basement, covered with cobwebs and possibly harboring rats and spiders. Think about it. What kinds of sights and sounds seem especially scary to *you*?

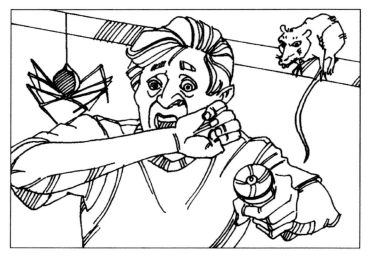

A. Describe each of the following places in a way that will scare your reader.

1. a very old, broken-down cottage: _____

_____

_____

_____

2. a cemetery at night: _____

_____

_____

_____

3. a dark attic or basement: _____

_____

_____

_____

4. a military battlefield: _____

_____

_____

_____

5. in the path of a hurricane: _____

_____

_____

_____

B. Choose one of the places you described in Part A, or one of the places listed in this box. Imagine that you had a very frightening experience there. Write a detailed description of what happened, how you managed to deal with it, and what you learned.

on a deserted island	at a zoo when an animal escapes
in a building that is on fire	in a boat during a storm at sea
in a bank during a robbery	skating on thin ice when it cracks
in a car when the brakes fail	on a stage when you have stage fright

_____

_____

_____

_____

_____

_____

_____

_____

_____

_____

_____

_____

_____

_____

_____

_____

_____

_____

_____

Commas

Writers use punctuation (commas, periods, question marks, etc.) to clarify the meaning of their sentences. A comma (,), for example, indicates a pause that is shorter than the pause at the end of a sentence.

> The comma is versatile; no other punctuation mark has so many uses. But by the same token, the majority of punctuation errors involve the comma.

Commas are properly used to:

- **set off introductory words, phrases, and clauses.**

  First, we must save some money.

  By working very hard, we finished the job.

  If what we hear is true, the concert will be canceled.

- **separate words, phrases, and clauses in a series.**

  Did you buy apples, bananas, and oranges?

  She raced into the house, ran upstairs, and took a fast shower.

  I came, I saw, I conquered.

- **separate the individual items in dates and addresses.**

  Lou graduated on June 10, 2002.

  The Lorcas live at 21 Park Street, Mountain View, California.

A. Add necessary commas to the following sentences.

1. To be certain of being heard Hal shouted out the answer.

2. Nonetheless everyone's attendance will be required.

3. Before moving to Seattle Jason bought an umbrella a raincoat and some heavy rubber boots.

4. Sam peeled the potatoes Roger sliced the onions and Earl chopped the carrots.

5. Having studied into the wee hours Kerry was almost too tired to take the test.

6. No later than April 15 2004 you must pay your income tax.

7. Suddenly the coach sent Spencer Anthony and Floyd into the game.

8. At your earliest opportunity tell the principal about the problem you've been having.

The comma is also used to:

• **separate two or more coordinate (equally forceful) adjectives before a noun.**

   a long, sleek, black limousine   *a skinny, dirty, lost dog*

• **set off interrupting words or phrases from the rest of the sentence.**

   Mrs. Green, carrying a bouquet of roses,   *Michael Jordan, a great athlete, played*
   greeted her mother at the airport.   *basketball for the Chicago Bulls.*

• **set off the designation of the speaker in direct quotations.**

   "Be sure," he advised, "to come home early."   *Virginia cried, "You can't make me do it!"*

B. Add necessary commas to the following sentences.

   1. I said "Come over here Julie and meet my new friend."

   2. If you want to visit the Louvre one of the world's finest museums you must go to Paris France.

   3. Drinking alcohol the cause of most auto accidents can easily become addictive.

   4. "Rosemary" he replied "is my beautiful younger sister."

   5. Ernie's old car on the other hand is not worth the cost of repair.

C. Write original, example sentences using commas as indicated.

   1. **TO SET OFF THE DESIGNATION OF THE SPEAKER IN A DIRECT QUOTATION:** _____

      _____

      _____

   2. **TO SEPARATE TWO OR MORE COORDINATE ADJECTIVES BEFORE A NOUN:** _____

      _____

      _____

   3. **TO SET OFF INTERRUPTING WORDS OR PHRASES FROM THE REST OF THE SENTENCE:** _____

      _____

      _____

   4. **TO SEPARATE WORDS, PHRASES, OR CLAUSES IN A SERIES:** _____

      _____

      _____

Lesson 13 — On Vacation

A vacation is always a welcome change of pace. It doesn't matter if you go on a trip or stick close to home. The main thing is that you get away from your regular routine and do something new.

A. Imagine a dream vacation. It might be one you've actually taken or one you've only dreamed about. Answer these questions about it.

1. Where did you go?

_____

2. Who went with you?

_____

3. Where did you stay?

_____

4. What did you do?

_____

_____

5. What new things did you eat?

_____

_____

6. What museums or other points of interest did you visit?

_____

_____

7. What did you buy or wish you could buy?

_____

_____

8. What advice would you give to someone who wanted to go there?

_____

_____

9. What was the highlight of your trip?

_____

_____

B. Now, write two postcards describing your vacation or special moments during your vacation. Write the first postcard to a relative. Write the second one to a friend.

TO:

TO:

Lesson 14 — Describing a Minor Event

Some events, like a parade on New Year's Day, can be considered major. Other events, the ordinary ones that make up most of our days, can be considered minor. In fact, even major events are made up of a series of minor events. The New Year's Day parade, for example, is preceded by the decorating of floats, the making of costumes, and the application of makeup.

A. Use your skill in descriptive writing to describe a minor event. Choose from the list of minor events in the box, or think of one of your own.

a sunrise	building a snowman	starting a campfire
a rainstorm	roasting marshmallows	making pancakes
washing a car	riding a bike in the park	raking leaves

Write your choice of minor events here: _____

Before you begin writing, answer the following questions about your chosen event:

1. What happens at the beginning of the minor event?

   _____

   _____

2. What sights are associated with this event?

   _____

   _____

3. What sounds might you hear as the event is occurring?

   _____

   _____

4. What smells might accompany the event?

   _____

   _____

5. What tastes might go along with the event?

   _____

   _____

6. Are any special textures associated with the event? If so, what are they?

_____

_____

7. How does the minor event progress?

_____

_____

8. What happens at the end?

_____

_____

B. Using your answers to the questions, write a paragraph about your minor event. Describe its sequence in detail. When you have finished your rough draft, revise your paragraph, after asking yourself questions like these:

- Did I use vivid nouns, verbs, adjectives, and adverbs?
- Did I use a variety of sentence structures?
- Did I include a topic sentence, detail sentences, and a concluding sentence?
- Will my reader be able to envision the minor event based on my description?

After making revisions based on these questions, write your final version on a separate sheet of paper.

Lesson 15 — Catalog Products

You can buy just about anything from a catalog. From furniture to vitamins, from baby clothes to kitchen supplies, from books to flower bulbs—the list is endless. In a catalog, the text is just as important as the pictures. The written descriptions of the products give the consumer the information he or she needs to make a decision. Think about the catalogs you have read. What kind of information were you looking for? Most likely, you wanted details about the products, such as sizes, dimensions, and prices.

Here is an example of a catalog entry:

OVERSIZED ROPE HAMMOCK

This is the sturdiest, most durable, and best-made hammock available. Unlike ordinary hammocks, it is handwoven instead of knotted. Only the highest-grade, softest cotton twill rope is used. In fact, this hammock contains twice as much rope as most. The two-person hammock uses a full 1,100 feet of rope. Handcrafted seasoned oak supports provide maximum stability. Hooks and chains are provided with instructions for hanging.

TWO-PERSON HAMMOCK. 5′ W x 7′ L.
Overall 13½′ L. 26300C $499.95
REGULAR-SIZE HAMMOCK: 4′ W x 6½′ L.
Overall 12′ L. 26302C $429.95

A. Catalog writers have two purposes: to give the buyer essential information and to sell the product. Imagine that you are a catalog writer. What information would be most important to include in a catalog entry for each of the following products?

1. a laptop computer: _____

    _____

2. a treadmill: _____

    _____

3. a hairdryer: _____

    _____

4. a table lamp: _____

    _____

5. a rocking horse: _____

    _____

B. Write a complete catalog entry for one of the products listed in Part A, or choose a product of your own. As you write, remember that you are trying to sell the product as well as give accurate information about it. Include a sketch of the product you are describing.

(NAME OF PRODUCT)

(PRODUCT SKETCH)

Figurative Language

In *figurative language*, the words used are not meant to be taken literally. Usually, figurative language states or implies a comparison of two unlike things. Using some figurative language is a good way to make your writing more colorful and interesting. Here are the four most common kinds of figurative language:

DEFINITION:		**EXAMPLE:**
A **simile** directly states a comparison between two unlike things, using the word *like* or *as*.	↔	The sunlight sparkled *like diamonds* on the cool blue lake.
Personification applies human qualities of behavior to nonhuman things.	↔	The sparkling lake *danced to the song of the wind*.
A **metaphor** implies a comparison between two unlike things by equating one with the other.	↔	The sunlight *was a sparkling diamond* on the cool blue lake.
Hyperbole uses exaggeration.	↔	A *million points of light* sparkled on the lake.

A. Identify the type of figurative language that is used in each of the following sentences.

1. _____ Melissa gained a ton of weight over the holidays.

2. _____ The well-oiled motor hummed happily along.

3. _____ The snow covered the ground like a warm comforter.

4. _____ The waves murmured sleepily.

5. _____ Sylvia runs like a gazelle.

6. _____ The young soldier fired the shot heard 'round the world.

7. _____ Dave's greeting was music to Susan's ears.

8. _____ The mirror had been Angela's friend up until now.

9. _____ Our friendship is as comfortable as an old bathrobe.

10. _____ Danielle was a rose among the thorns of Fred's acquaintances.

11. _____ I cried a river over you.

12. _____ The autumn of Jim's life began with his sixtieth birthday.

B. As directed, write examples of **similes, metaphors, personifications,** and **hyperboles** for each of the 12 items below.

———— SIMILE ————

1. a waterfall

   _____

   _____

   _____

2. a baby's cry

   _____

   _____

   _____

3. a ticking clock

   _____

   _____

   _____

———— PERSONIFICATION ————

7. a tree

   _____

   _____

   _____

8. a cat

   _____

   _____

   _____

9. a chair

   _____

   _____

   _____

———— METAPHOR ————

4. a friendship

   _____

   _____

   _____

5. someone's eyes

   _____

   _____

   _____

6. a house

   _____

   _____

   _____

———— HYPERBOLE ————

10. speed

   _____

   _____

   _____

11. cost

   _____

   _____

   _____

12. food

   _____

   _____

   _____

Lesson 16 — Sales Brochure

The purpose of a sales brochure is, of course, to sell a product or a service. Unlike a catalog, the description is very detailed. For example, a sales brochure about a housing development might include floor plans and descriptions of luxurious extras. It might also include a blurb about the builder and information about the neighborhood. Some brochures even feature quotations from happy customers who are satisfied with the product.

COWABUNGA, DUDE!

A. Choose one of the products or services listed in the box, or make up one of your own. Then jot down some ideas for information you might include in a sales brochure for that item.

a skateboard	**a backpack**	**spa services**	**building blocks for toddlers**
an automobile	**a surfboard**	**a cell phone**	**software for a computer game**

1. Name and describe the product or service.

   _____

   _____

2. Tell something about the company that manufactures the product or provides the service.

   _____

   _____

3. Tell why this product or service is better than those offered by competitors.

   _____

   _____

4. Tell the customer how he or she can pay for the product or service. For example, do you accept credit cards? Do you have easy-payment plans?

   _____

   _____

5. What have some satisfied customers said about the product or service?

   _____

   _____

B. Now, write copy for a two-sided sales brochure describing the product or service you've chosen. Expand on your answers from Part A. Then, on a separate sheet of paper, sketch out your brochure, inserting art where appropriate.

COPY FOR FRONT OF BROCHURE:

_____

_____

_____

_____

_____

_____

_____

_____

_____

_____

_____

COPY FOR BACK OF BROCHURE:

_____

_____

_____

_____

_____

_____

_____

_____

_____

_____

Lesson 17
Sensory Descriptions

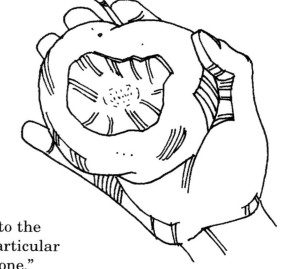

It may be impossible to write descriptively without appealing to at least one of the senses. Many things, in fact, can be described in terms of more than one sense. For example, you can appreciate an apple with all five senses. You can see that it is red or shiny or round. You can hear a crisp, crunching sound as you bite into it. You can taste a juicy sweetness or tartness. You can also smell the apple, and touch it to feel its smooth surface.

A. Complete the chart with words that appeal to the senses. A few have been done for you. If a particular sense is *not* used in any given case, write "none."

	SIGHT	HEARING	SMELL	TASTE	TOUCH
fire		crackling			
orchids			sweet		
fish					
computer					
rainbow	colorful				
ocean				salty	
forest					
snow					cold
wind					

B. Choose one of the items listed on the chart in Part A, or make up one of your own. Write a paragraph describing the item. Be sure to use words that engage all the senses that apply to that item. When you finish, exchange papers with a classmate. Offer and accept criticism that will improve your work. Use this checklist as a guide:

1. Have I used language that helps the reader imagine seeing, hearing, tasting, smelling, or touching the item?

2. Have I used appropriate transition words to make my sentences flow well?

3. Have I spelled all the words correctly?

4. Are my sentences punctuated correctly?

5. Have I corrected any mistakes in grammar?

6. Have I used a variety of sentence types? That is, do I have a pleasing variety of simple, compound, and complex sentences?

Describing Seasons: Winter and Summer

Some seasonal changes occur everywhere. These changes might be quite dramatic—with triple-digit temperatures in the summer and deep snow in the winter. If you live in a more temperate climate, the changes may be subtle—with only slight variations in temperature or a bit more rain.

Every mile is two in winter.

A. Think about winter and summer in an area you know well. Write a brief description of each of the following aspects of the seasons.

1. winter weather: _____

   _____

2. summer weather: _____

   _____

3. plant life in the winter: _____

   _____

4. plant life in the summer: _____

   _____

5. animal behavior in the winter: _____

   _____

6. animal behavior in the summer: _____

   _____

7. clothes you wear in the winter: _____

   _____

8. clothes you wear in the summer: _____

   _____

9. your winter activities: _____

   _____

10. your summer activities: _____

   _____

B. Now, write a descriptive paragraph about winter or summer. Pick and choose from the information you provided in Part A, and add any other information that you think fits. When you have finished your rough draft, revise your work based on this checklist:

1. Is my paragraph mechanically correct (spelling, grammar, punctuation)?

2. Did I use vivid nouns, verbs, adjectives, and adverbs?

3. Did I vary the lengths and types (simple, compound, complex) of my sentences?

4. Are there any places where I can improve the flow of my paragraph by adding transitional words and phrases?

Verb Voices

English verbs have two voices: *active* and *passive.*

• **When the subject *performs* the action, the verb is in the active voice.**

Brandon washes the window.	*Mia drew a picture.*	*The gardener mows the grass.*

The active voice is direct and forceful.

• **When the subject *receives* the action, the verb is in the passive voice.**

The window is washed by Brandon.	*A picture was drawn by Mia.*	*The grass is mowed by the gardener.*

The passive voice can make sentences confusing and unnecessarily wordy. Avoid using the passive voice, except:

• **when the performer of the action is unknown or better left unidentified.**	• **when you want to emphasize the receiver rather than the performer of the action.**
The crime was reported by an anonymous caller.	*An unfortunate error was made.*

A. Write **A** or **P** to show whether each item below is in the *active* or *passive* voice.

1. _____ I included pictures.

2. _____ Pictures are included.

3. _____ They will set the date.

4. _____ The date will be set.

5. _____ The team is coached by her.

6. _____ She coaches the team.

7. _____ Comfort was offered by Eli.

8. _____ Eli offered comfort.

B. Study the example sentences. Then write **T** or **F** to show whether each statement below is *true* or *false.*

1. _____ Active verbs occur in a subject-verb-object pattern.

2. _____ The use of passive verbs is technically correct.

3. _____ If you don't want to reveal who did something, use an active-voice verb.

4. _____ Passive-voice verbs usually make sentence meaning more accessible and immediate.

C. First, write **A** or **P** to identify the verb in each sentence as *active* or *passive*. Then rewrite the sentences, making the active voice passive or the passive voice active. The first one has been done for you.

1. _P_   Thousands of packages are received by people every day.

   People receive thousands of packages every day.

2. _____   Abraham Lincoln called the fallen soldier a great patriot.

   _____

   _____

3. _____   The doors are closed five minutes after class begins.

   _____

   _____

4. _____   The lost watch was returned by the man who found it.

   _____

   _____

5. _____   The committee carefully considered your complaint.

   _____

   _____

6. _____   Some personality traits are easily observed by psychologists.

   _____

   _____

7. _____   Great benefits are offered to employees by that furniture company.

   _____

   _____

8. _____   The superintendent hired the principal of our school.

   _____

   _____

Lesson 19 — Describing Seasons: Fall and Spring

Fall and spring are transitional seasons. They bridge the gap between more extreme seasons. But a colder snap in the air isn't the only way to tell fall from spring. To write an interesting description, you will have to include information about many aspects of the season.

April showers bring May flowers.

A. Think about fall and spring in an area you know well. Write a brief description of each of the following aspects of the seasons.

1. fall weather: _____

2. spring weather: _____

3. plant life in the fall: _____

4. plant life in the spring: _____

5. animal behavior in the fall: _____

6. animal behavior in the spring: _____

7. fall clothes: _____

8. spring clothes: _____

9. favorite fall activities: _____

10. favorite spring activities: _____

B. Now, write a descriptive paragraph about fall or spring. Pick and choose from the information you provided in Part A, and add any other information that you think fits. When you've finished your rough draft, revise your work based on this checklist:

1. Mechanics: Are spelling, grammar, and punctuation correct?

2. Word choice: Are nouns, verbs, adjectives, and adverbs vivid?

3. Sentence variety: Did I vary my sentence types and lengths?

4. Transitions: Did I use effective transitional words and phrases?

How could you best describe a city your readers have never seen? If your description was limited to one paragraph, you'd have to choose your words carefully. Which details would be most interesting to your reader? Which details would you decide to leave out?

A. Study these facts about Paris, France. Circle five key details that, in your judgment, would give your readers the most enjoyable "armchair travel" experience. Then write your descriptive paragraph on the lines below.

- The Seine River crosses the city from east to west.
- The 984-ft. Eiffel Tower is a truly spectacular sight.
- Flower stands dot the city's wide, tree-lined boulevards.
- Once the residence of French kings, the Louvre now houses the world's largest art museum.
- The Arc de Triomphe symbolizes national honor to all Frenchmen.
- Paris is one of the most crowded cities in the world.
- Tourists take boat trips through the city's ancient underground sewers.
- Lovely public gardens are scattered throughout the city.
- The Palace of the Louvre is an excellent example of French architecture.
- Notre Dame Cathedral is the city's most famous church.
- Fine French food is available at sidewalk cafes as well as in world-famous restaurants.
- Covering 185 square miles, Paris lies 110 miles southeast of the English Channel.
- The French parliament meets in the beautiful Luxembourg Palace.

_____

_____

_____

_____

_____

_____

_____

_____

_____

_____

_____

_____

_____

B. Now do some research of your own on any foreign city of your choosing. Consult an encyclopedia or use the Internet to help you gather some facts about that city. Write your list of facts on the lines below.

- _____

- _____

- _____

- _____

- _____

- _____

- _____

- _____

- _____

- _____

C. Decide which facts you will use, and then write a first draft of your paragraph on the lines. To complete the process, check your paragraph to be sure that your spelling, grammar, and punctuation are correct. Write your revision on a separate sheet of paper.

_____

_____

_____

_____

_____

_____

_____

_____

_____

_____

_____

Fun with Hyperbole

Hyperbole, or extreme exaggeration, is often used for humorous effect. Let's have some fun with hyperbole!

A. Complete each of the following sentences with an image that is highly unlikely in real life but is very funny to think about.

EXAMPLE:

The sun was so hot that we could fry eggs on the sidewalk.

1. It was so cold that _____.

2. The wind was so strong that _____.

3. That family is so big that _____.

4. The traffic was so bad that _____.

5. He ate so much that _____.

6. We danced so fast that _____.

7. Her cookies are so delicious that _____.

8. The book is so interesting that _____.

9. The lake was so deep that _____.

10. That child is so smart that _____.

11. I studied so hard that _____.

12. The carpet was so thick that _____.

13. The music was so loud that _____.

14. It rained so hard that _____.

15. She is so tall that _____.

16. He is so sensitive that _____.

17. She cried so much that _____.

18. He laughed so hard that _____.

B. Write a paragraph describing each of the following situations, using hyperbole for humorous effect.

1. A woman starts knitting a muffler for herself, but she doesn't quite know when to stop.

_____

_____

_____

_____

_____

2. A man adds too much yeast to a bread recipe.

_____

_____

_____

_____

_____

3. A woman puts too much detergent in the washing machine.

_____

_____

_____

_____

_____

C. Now use hyperbole to develop an idea of your own. Write your paragraph on the lines below.

_____

_____

_____

_____

_____

_____

The Writing Process: Developing Ideas

Do you want to keep your readers interested in your ideas? Of course you do! How can you achieve your goal? First, develop your ideas so clearly that they're easy to understand. This always involves supplying specific details, examples, or reasons. Often it also means choosing a method of development that works well with your topic. The box below contains several good methods of development.

✔ **Time:** describing events or steps in the order of their occurrence

✔ **Space:** describing a city, for example, from outskirts to center or a mural from left to right

✔ **Increasing complexity:** beginning with the simple or familiar and going on to the more complex or unfamiliar

✔ **Comparison and contrast:** beginning with a discussion of the features of two ideas and ending by drawing a conclusion about the two

✔ **Support:** beginning with a general statement and going on to support it with specific examples, details, and reasons

✔ **Climax:** beginning with a specific fact or situation and continuing with more facts about the subject, ending with the most exciting moment or result

---

A. Think about each of the following topics. Then choose the most appropriate method of development. Write the method on the line. If more than one method would work, list them both.

1. Arrangements for a Wedding _____

2. The Dinosaur Exhibit at the
   Natural History Museum _____

3. The Development of the
   Polio Vaccine _____

4. How a Frog Develops _____

5. Public School or Private School—
   Which Is Better for You? _____

6. Wind Instruments from
   Whistles to Bassoons _____

7. The Battle of Antietam _____

8. Our New Home _____

9. Why Study Foreign Languages? _____

10. American and French Films _____

11. Central Park at Dawn _____

12. Divorce Is Increasing _____

13. A Trip Through the Grand Canyon _____

14. The Discovery of King Tut's Tomb _____

15. Training a Dog _____

B. Write one topic that would best lend itself to each of the following methods of development.

1. **Time:** _____

2. **Space:** _____

3. **Increasing complexity:** _____

4. **Support:** _____

5. **Climax:** _____

C. Now choose one topic and develop it in two or three paragraphs.

_____

_____

_____

_____

_____

_____

_____

_____

_____

_____

_____

_____

_____

_____

_____

_____

_____

A Memorable Experience

Think about a memorable experience you've had or heard about. Then follow these steps to write a description of it.

1. **Prewriting: Choose a Point of View**

   FIRST-PERSON: Are you writing about an experience you had yourself? If so, you will be writing from the first-person point of view. That means you will use the pronouns *I, me, my, mine,* and *myself.*

   THIRD-PERSON: Are you writing about an experience someone else told you about? If so, you are writing from the third-person point of view. You will refer to the main character—the one having the experience—with third-person pronouns such as *he* or *she.*

   Briefly describe the memorable experience on the lines below:

   _____

   _____

   _____

   _____

   _____

2. **Prewriting: Gathering Details**

   Before writing your first draft, gather details for your description. One good way to do this is to brainstorm. Close your eyes and relive the experience in your mind. Then jot down phrases to describe different phases of the experience. List adjectives and adverbs that would be appropriate in your description. Make word webs for each sense that was stimulated by the experience. For example, suppose you are describing an evening when a major league record was set at a ball game. A word web based on the sense of sight might look like this:

hot dog vendors

cheering crowd

runner on third base

SIGHTS

pitcher winding up

batter ready to strike

umpire behind home plate

Make your own word web based on your memorable experience:

3. **Prewriting: Organizing Information**

Now, put your details in order. Would it be most effective to relate the experience in the sequence in which it happened? Or would a different method of organization work better? As an alternative, you might consider comparison and contrast or a general statement followed by supporting details.

Write your method of organization here: _____

4. **Drafting**

After deciding on a method of organization, you can begin a first draft of your description. As you write, follow these tips:

- Try to keep your memorable experience fresh in your mind. Imagine that you are there *right now*. What colorful or unusual details pop out at you?

- Get your ideas down on paper quickly. Don't worry about every little detail of mechanics. You can polish your work later.

- First, write a strong opening that captures your readers' attention.

- Then write the body of your paper, developing your description by using sensory details.

- If appropriate, add any dialogue that might have been spoken during the experience. This will give a liveliness to your description and help your reader imagine being there with you.

- Write an effective conclusion. You might summarize the event with an inspiring observation about the experience, or conclude with a statement about how it made you feel.

5. **Revising and Editing**

   After noting areas that need improvement, revise your work. Ask yourself questions like these:

   - Is it easy for the reader to imagine what the experience was like?

   - Does the style of the writing match the experience in mood?

   - Is the description well-organized?

   - Within paragraphs in the body, are all topic sentences clear and well-supported by details?

   - Can transitional words and phrases be added to improve the flow of the story?

6. Give your narrative to a peer and invite him or her to review it. Offer to do the same for your peer. By offering and accepting input, you improve your chances of writing an excellent description.

7. Proofread your work. Make sure that your spelling, grammar, and mechanics are correct. These kinds of mistakes can be distracting to your reader.

8. **Make a final copy and publish it.**

   You can publish your description in many ways. Here are some ideas:

   - Read your paper orally.

   - With a small group, act out the events you have described.

   - Post a copy on a bulletin board in the classroom or an electronic bulletin board.

   - Write an e-mail to your friends, attaching a copy of your description.

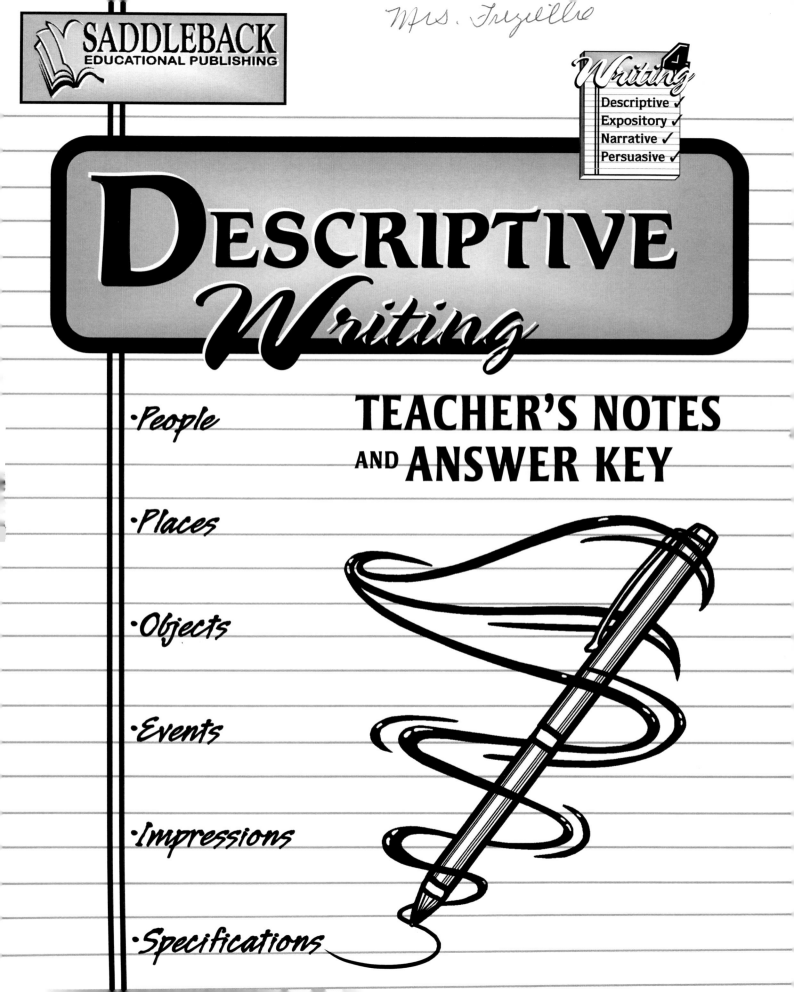

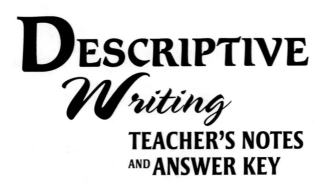

DESCRIPTIVE Writing
TEACHER'S NOTES
AND ANSWER KEY

— Writing 4 TITLES —

Descriptive Writing

Expository Writing

Narrative Writing

Persuasive Writing

SADDLEBACK
EDUCATIONAL PUBLISHING

Three Watson
Irvine, CA 92618-2767

Website: www.sdlback.com

Copyright © 2005 by Saddleback Educational Publishing. All rights reserved. No part of this book may be reproduced in any form or by any means, electronic or mechanical, including photocopying, recording, or by any information storage and retrieval system, without the written permission of the publisher.

ISBN-13: 978-1-56254-755-4
ISBN-10: 1-56254-755-0
eBook: 978-1-60291-548-0

Printed in the United States of America
12 11 10 09 08   9 8 7 6 5 4 3

"Practice is the best of all instructors."

—Publilius Syrus, *Maxim*

Let's face it: *Most* students need to improve their writing skills.

All too often, student work is blemished by poorly composed sentences, misspelled words, and punctuation errors. The meaning the student writer intended to convey is unclear, if not downright confusing. What's the solution? The venerable old Roman got it right more than 2,000 years ago: practice, practice, and more practice!

Saddleback's WRITING 4 series links writing to purpose. Each of the four workbooks—NARRATIVE, EXPOSITORY, DESCRIPTIVE, and PERSUASIVE—specifically focuses on one particular "reason for writing." Each workbook contains 21 applications lessons and seven basic skills practice lessons. Relevant applications include drafting personal and business letters, narrating an historical event, and reviewing a movie. Specific skills taught include analyzing your audience, recognizing propaganda, creating tone, and sorting fact and opinion. Fundamental skills and concepts such as main idea, supporting details, and writing introductions and conclusions are reviewed in all four workbooks.

ONGOING ASSESSMENT

Periodic checks of student workbooks are highly recommended. If possible, assign peer tutors to coach remediation.

LESSON EXTENSIONS

To reinforce and enrich the workbook exercises, you may want to assign "extra credit" activities such as the following:

▶ write step-by-step instructions for some task that individual students know how to do, e.g., make a salad, repair a flat tire, etc.

▶ record the stories they write, or read them aloud to students in other classrooms

▶ write independent descriptions of the same event or object; then compare and contrast, discussing viewpoint, vocabulary, and level of detail

▶ bring in "letters to the editor" from newspapers and magazines to analyze and discuss in class

▶ write employment reference letters for each other

▶ critique TV commercials or ads they've seen in the print media

▶ write directions for walking or driving from one point to another, e.g., home to school, library to home, etc.

▶ interview a parent or a school employee, and then "write up" the interview for an article in the school newspaper

For most lessons, answers will vary widely. When evaluating students' answers and descriptions, look for accuracy and creativity in following the prompts. Some lessons require specific answers, as follows:

LESSON 3: Using Vivid Adjectives (pp. 10–11)

The following adjectives should be circled:

A. 1. shimmery, pastel

2. large, red, round

3. bright, blue, delicate, white

4. tiny, white

B. 1. noisy, fragrant

2. hungry, spicy

3. tired, festive

4. quiet, mournful

Rewritten sentences should present sharply contrasting images.

**BASIC SKILLS PRACTICE: Developing an Outline
(pp. 12–13)**

A. An outline is simply a <u>plan</u>. It helps you organize your <u>thoughts</u> in the most effective <u>order</u>. The better your outline, the easier it will be to write your first <u>draft</u>.

Outlines vary with the <u>type</u> of writing you are doing. An appropriate outline for a research project would be quite <u>structured</u> and <u>detailed</u>. For a one-page business letter, a fairly <u>brief</u> and <u>sketchy</u> outline will usually be adequate. But whether your outline is long or short, it will always set out the major <u>topics</u> and the supporting <u>details</u> for each topic.

<u>Review</u> your outline after you complete it. Be flexible. You may want to <u>rearrange</u> the major sections or add something you didn't think of the first time around. Once you're satisfied that the major and <u>minor</u> points are covered, you are ready to <u>write</u>.

B. 1. T   2. T   3. T   4. F

C.   Finding a Job

  I. Part-time jobs

    A. Hearing about jobs from friends

    B. Newspaper classified ads

  II. Applying for the job

    A. Over the telephone

    B. Letter of application

  III. The interview

    A. Creating the proper image

    B. Arriving on time

D. Student outlines will vary.

LESSON 4: Using Vivid Adverbs (pp. 14–15)

The following adverbs should be circled:

A. 1. gracefully

2. afterwards

3. breathlessly, late

4. broke, consequently

B. 1. biweekly

2. extremely

3. hardly

4. skillfully

Rewritten sentences should present sharply contrasting images.

BASIC SKILLS PRACTICE: Sentence Structure (pp. 20–21)

A. 1. T   2. F   3. T   4. F   5. F
6. T   7. T   8. T   9. F   10. F

B. Answers will vary. Possible answers:

1. The cat was frustrated when the mouse it was chasing ran into a hole in the wall.
   STRUCTURE: complex

2. When Bill answered the ringing telephone, he found that the caller was his girlfriend.
   STRUCTURE: complex

3. In April, Nicole and Brad plan to take a vacation in Japan.
   STRUCTURE: complex

4. The store was very crowded, and one customer was irate because she'd been waiting in line for 20 minutes.
   STRUCTURE: compound-complex

C. Answers will vary.

BASIC SKILLS PRACTICE: Usage: Formal and Informal English (pp. 28–29)

A. 1. formal English

2. informal English

3. formal English

4. informal English

5. formal English

6. informal English

7. formal English

8. formal English

BASIC SKILLS PRACTICE: Commas (pp. 36–37)

A. The following sentences show proper placement of commas:

1. To be certain of being heard, Hal shouted out the answer.

2. Nonetheless, everyone's attendance will be required.

3. Before moving to Seattle, Jason bought an umbrella, a raincoat, and some heavy rubber boots.

4. Sam peeled the potatoes, Roger sliced the onions, and Earl chopped the carrots.

5. Having studied into the wee hours, Kerry was almost too tired to take the test.

6. No later than April 15, 2004, you must pay your income tax.

7. Suddenly, the coach sent Spencer, Anthony, and Floyd into the game.

8. At your earliest opportunity, tell the principal about the problem you've been having.

B. The following sentences show proper placement of commas:

1. I said, "Come over here, Julie, and meet my new friend."

2. If you want to visit the Louvre, one of the world's finest museums, you must go to Paris, France.

3. Drinking alcohol, the cause of most auto accidents, can easily become addictive.

4. "Rosemary," he replied, "is my beautiful, younger sister."

5. Ernie's old car, on the other hand, is not worth the cost of repair.

C. Answers will vary, but make sure student sentences have commas placed in the manner directed.

BASIC SKILLS PRACTICE: Figurative Language (pp. 44–45)

A. 1. hyperbole

2. personification

3. simile

4. personification

5. simile

6. hyperbole

7. metaphor

8. personification

9. simile

10. metaphor

11. hyperbole

12. metaphor

BASIC SKILLS PRACTICE: Verb Voices (pp. 52–53)

A. 1. A   2. P   3. A   4. P
      5. P   6. A   7. P   8. A

B. 1. T   2. T   3. F   4. F

C. 2. A — The fallen soldier was called a great patriot by Abraham Lincoln.

3. P — They close the doors five minutes after class begins.

4. P — The man who found the lost watch returned it.

5. A — Your complaint was carefully considered by the committee.

6. P — Psychologists can easily observe some personality traits.

7. P — That furniture company offers great benefits to its employees.

8. A — The principal of our school was hired by the superintendent.

BASIC SKILLS PRACTICE: The Writing Process: Developing Ideas (pp. 60–61)

A. Accept any answers students can support. Sample answers are given.

1. comparison and contrast (if you're trying to sell a service to a bride) or space (if you're describing a particular wedding arrangement)

2. space

3. time (if describing the steps taken in the development of the vaccine) or climax (if leading up to the dramatic result of a polio vaccine)

4. time

5. comparison and contrast

6. increasing complexity

7. time

8. space

9. support

10. comparison and contrast

11. space

12. support

13. time

14. climax

15. increasing complexity

ISBN-13: 978-1-56254-755-4
ISBN-10: 1-56254-755-0

90000

9 781562 547554